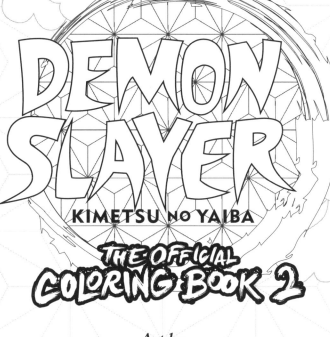

DEMON SLAYER

KIMETSU NO YAIBA

THE OFFICIAL COLORING BOOK 2

Art by

KOYOHARU GOTOUGE

KOYOHARU GOTOUGE

Hello! I'm Gotouge. I've put out another coloring book. I hope you enjoy it.

Ever since I was a child, I've never been very good at coloring, so I often found myself quitting halfway through. I also remember being shocked when I would see my friends' beautifully colored drawings. How about all of you?

Here are some tips:

+ Start with lighter colors and light shading.
+ Adjust the shade by layering the same color.
+ Do your best to color evenly.
+ Be careful to stay within the lines.

Above all, the key to coloring is believing in yourself and never giving up.

It might be fun to try coloring Tanjiro and his friends in different colors than usual. I will also give it a try with my Coupy-Pencils and colored pencils!

THANK YOU!

**DEMON SLAYER: KIMETSU NO YAIBA
THE OFFICIAL COLORING BOOK 2**

Shonen Jump Edition

Art by
KOYOHARU GOTOUGE

KIMETSU NO YAIBA NURIE CHO - DAIDAI/AI -
© 2021 by Koyoharu Gotouge
All rights reserved.
First published in Japan in 2021 by SHUEISHA Inc., Tokyo.
English translation rights arranged by SHUEISHA Inc.

DESIGN Yukiko Whitley   **EDITOR** David Brothers

The stories, characters, and incidents mentioned in this publication are entirely fictional.

No portion of this book may be reproduced or transmitted in any form or by any means without written permission from the copyright holders.

Printed in the U.S.A.

Published by VIZ Media, LLC
P.O. Box 77010
San Francisco, CA 94107

10 9 8 7 6 5 4 3 2 1
First printing, May 2023

ISBN: 978-1-9747-3897-7

VIZ MEDIA
viz.com

SHONEN JUMP

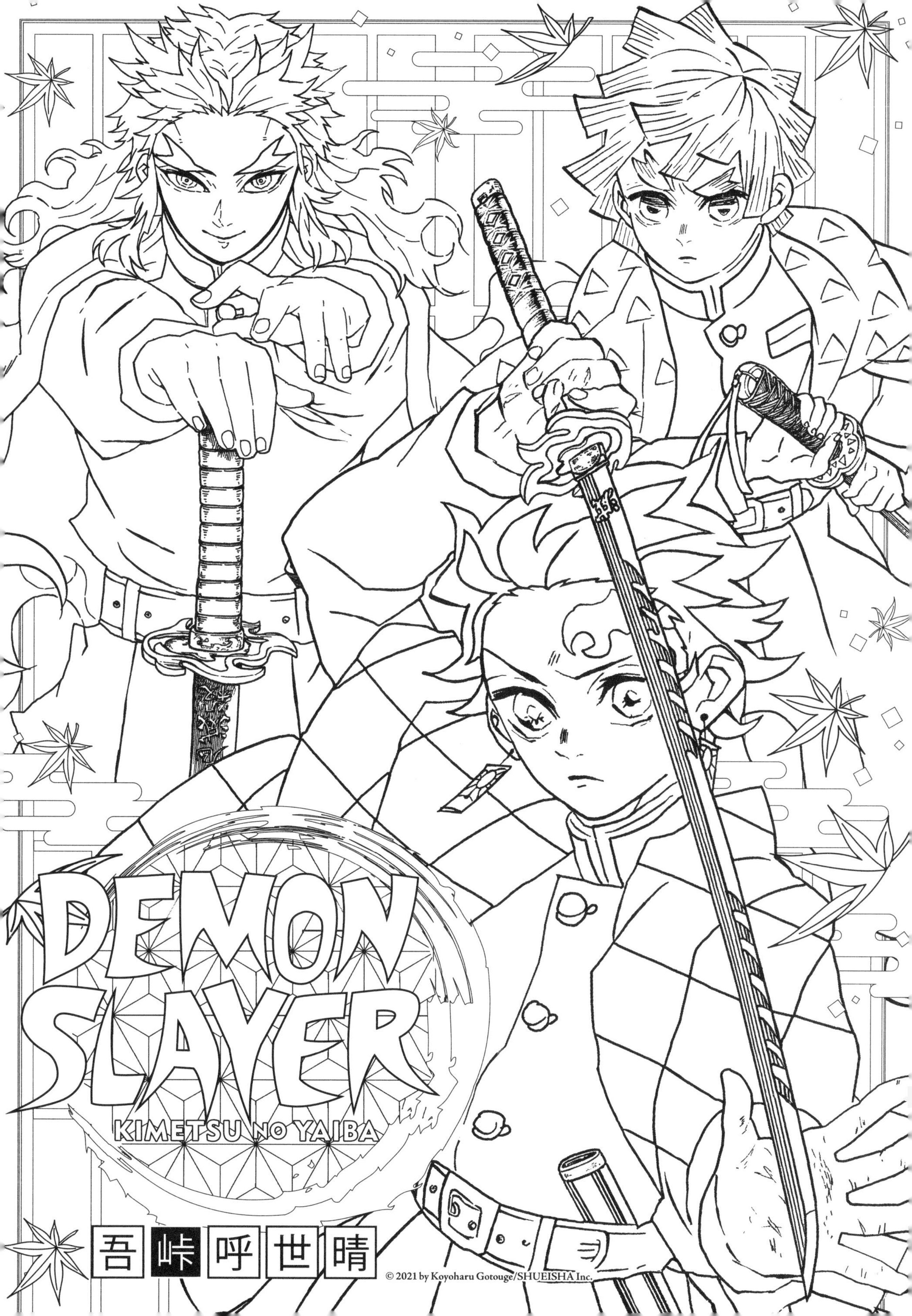
DEMON SLAYER
KIMETSU NO YAIBA
吾峠呼世晴

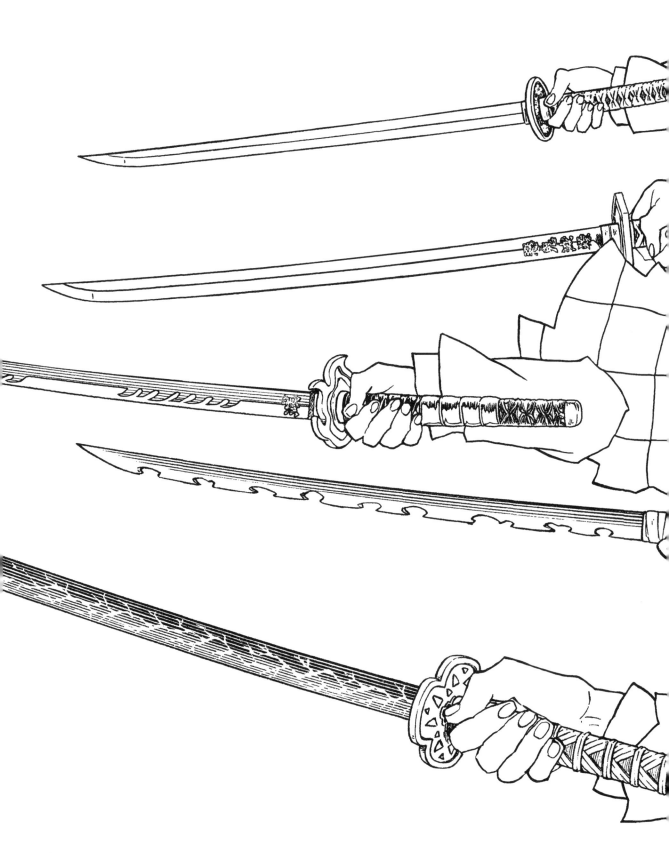

© 2021 by Koyoharu Gotouge/SHUEISHA Inc.

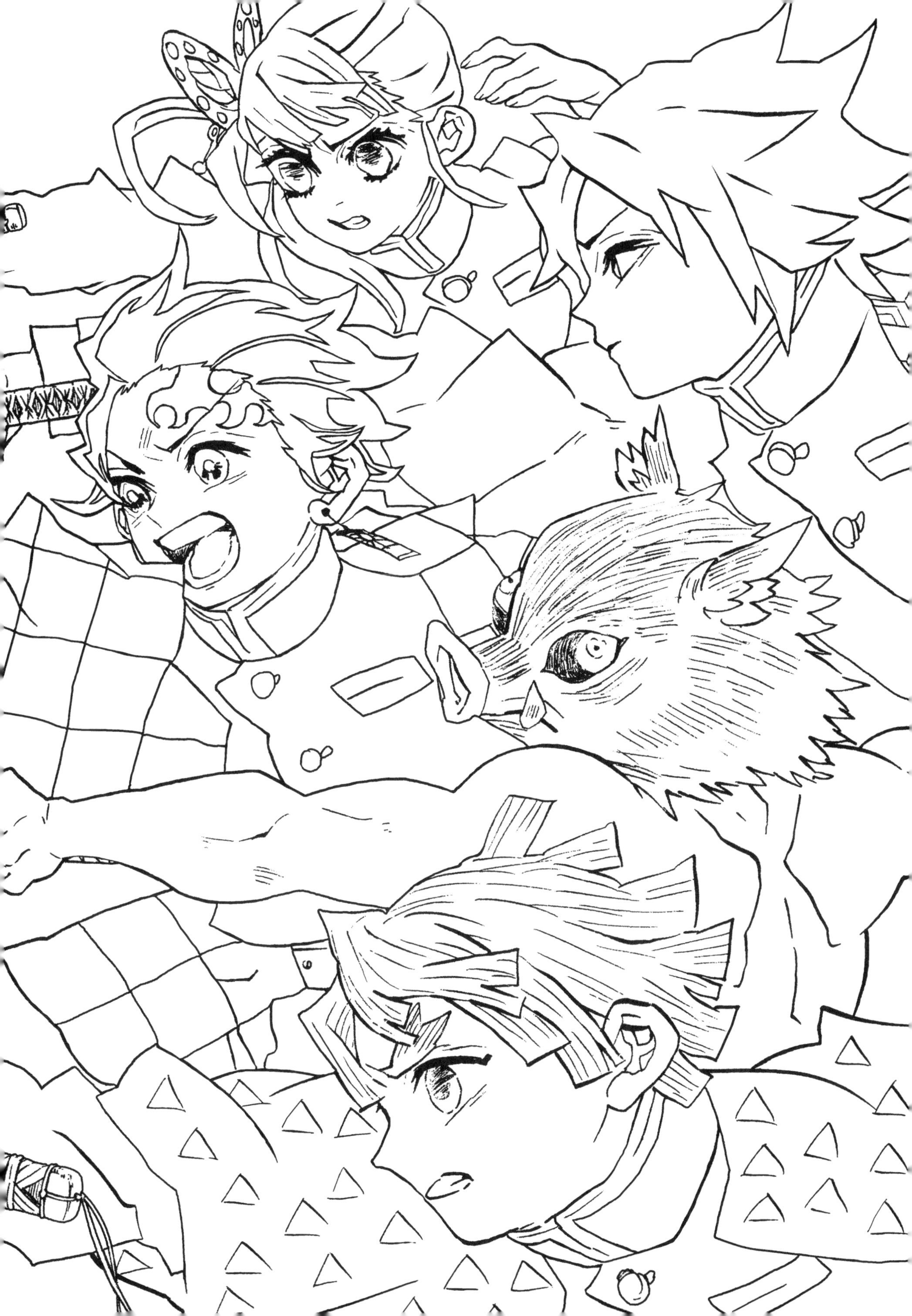

© 2021 by Koyoharu Gotouge/SHUEISHA Inc.

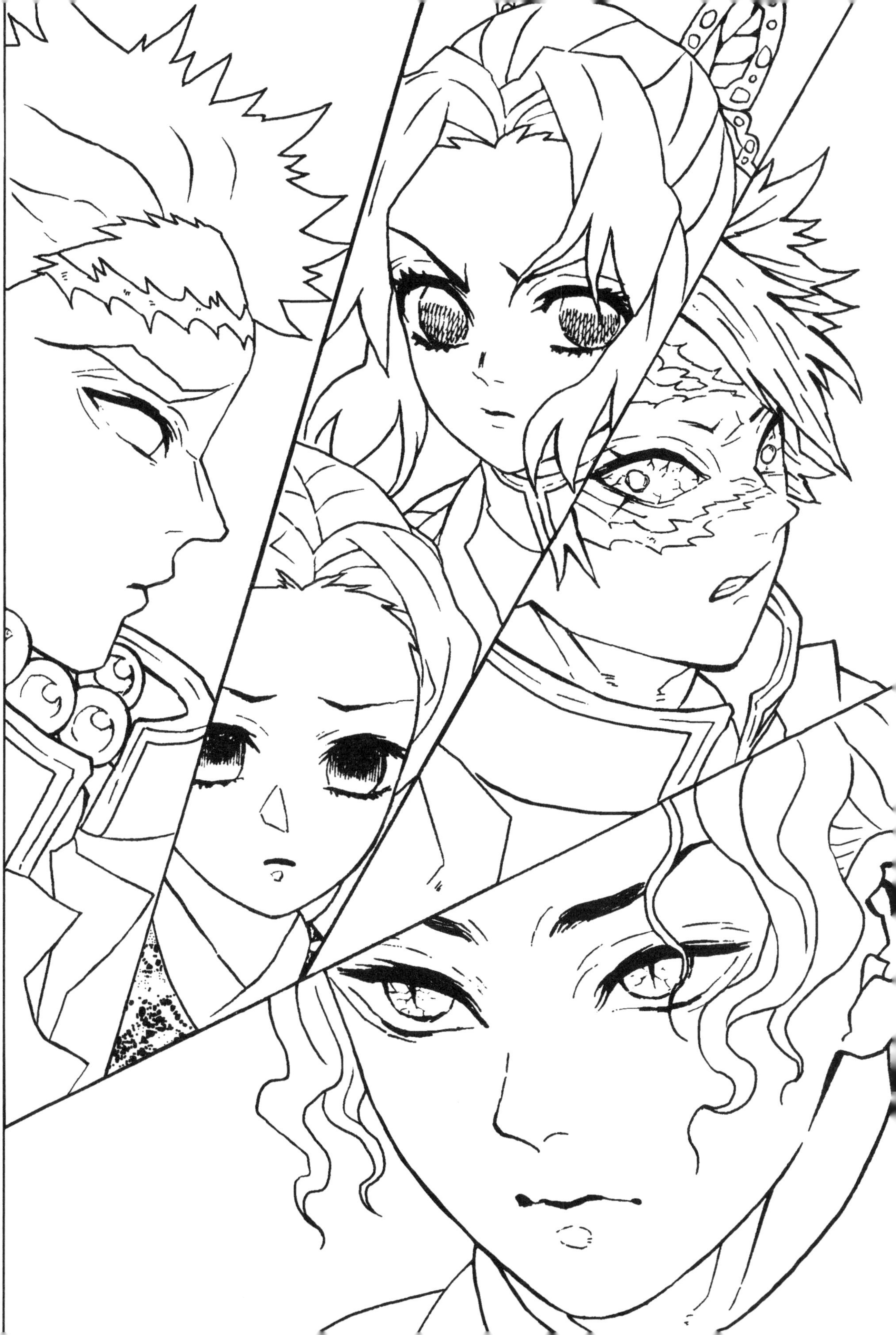

© 2021 by Koyoharu Gotouge/SHUEISHA Inc.

© 2021 by Koyoharu Gotouge/SHUEISHA Inc.

© 2021 by Koyoharu Gotouge/SHUEISHA Inc.

© 2021 by Koyoharu Gotouge/SHUEISHA Inc.

KANAO TSUYURI.

© 2021 by Koyoharu Gotouge/SHUEISHA Inc.

© 2021 by Koyoharu Gotouge/SHUEISHA Inc.

© 2021 by Koyoharu Gotouge/SHUEISHA Inc.

© 2021 by Koyoharu Gotouge/SHUEISHA Inc.
Text is read right to left.

AND IT WAS HARD TO SENSE IT!

BLOOD DEMON ART WAS HIDING THAT HUGE THING!!

HOW-EVER...

...IF YOU BARE YOUR FANGS AT INNOCENT PEOPLE...

© 2021 by Koyoharu Gotouge/SHUEISHA Inc.
Text is read right to left.

...WILL BURN YOU TO THE BONE!!

...MY BRIGHT RED FLAME BLADE...

© 2021 by Koyoharu Gotouge/SHUEISHA Inc.

I WILL PROTECT YOU, NEZUKO.

ZZZ

NGAH...

I WILL PROM-MMBLE...

© 2021 by Koyoharu Gotouge/SHUEISHA Inc.
Text is read right to left.

© 2021 by Koyoharu Gotouge/SHUEISHA Inc.

水の呼吸　陸ノ型

ねじれ渦

© 2021 by Koyoharu Gotouge/SHUEISHA Inc.

KAMADO!

RENGOKU!

© 2021 by Koyoharu Gotouge/SHUEISHA Inc.
Text is read right to left.

© 2021 by Koyoharu Gotouge/SHUEISHA Inc.

破壊殺・羅針

術式展開

IF YOU WON'T BECOME A DEMON, THEN I'LL HAVE TO KILL YOU.

© 2021 by Koyoharu Gotouge/SHUEISHA Inc.

© 2021 by Koyoharu Gotouge/SHUEISHA Inc.

© 2021 by Koyoharu Gotouge/SHUEISHA Inc.

© 2021 by Koyoharu Gotouge/SHUEISHA Inc.

© 2021 by Koyoharu Gotouge/SHUEISHA Inc.

© 2021 by Koyoharu Gotouge/SHUEISHA Inc.

© 2021 by Koyoharu Gotouge/SHUEISHA Inc.

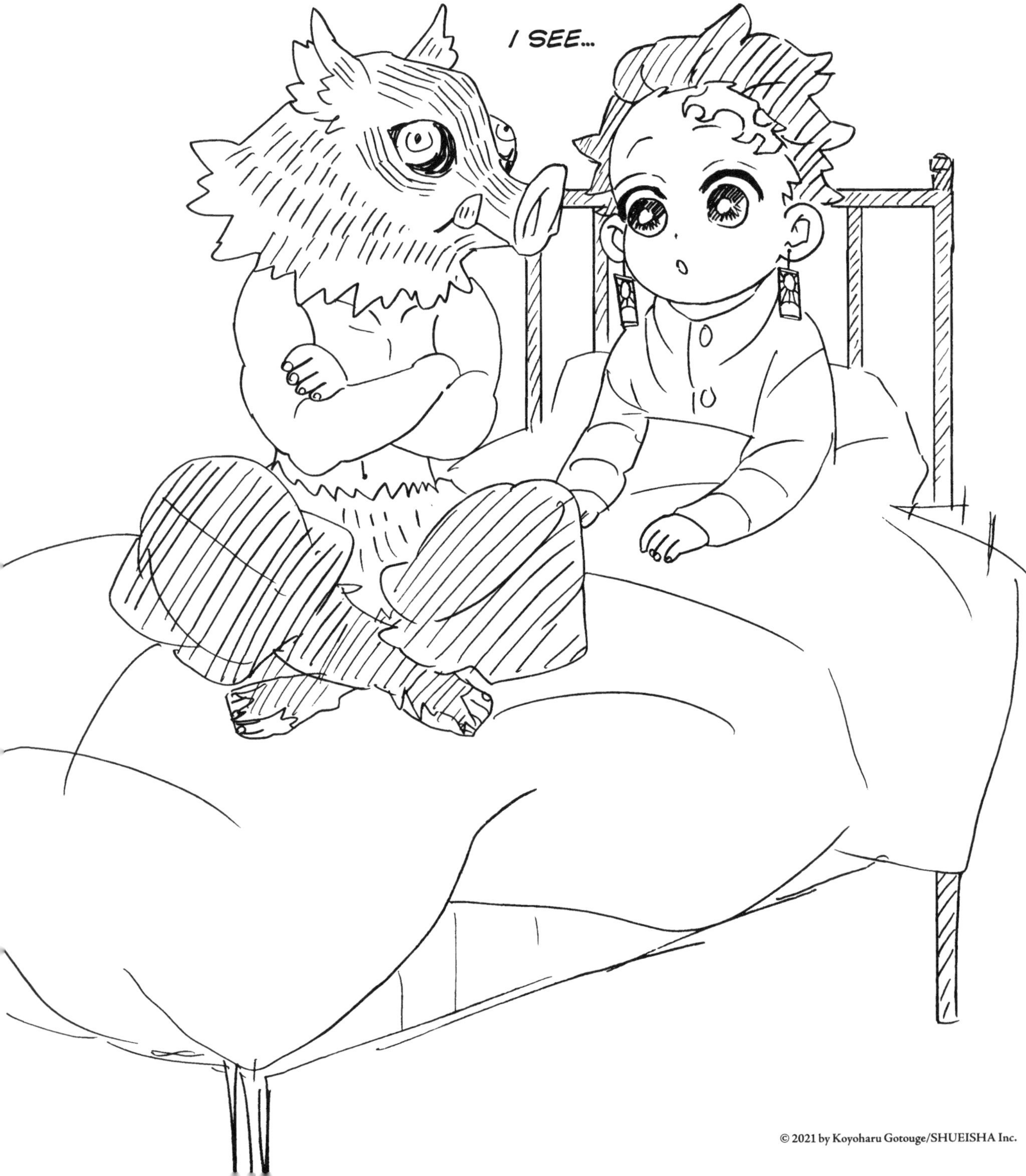
I SEE...

© 2021 by Koyoharu Gotouge/SHUEISHA Inc.

© 2021 by Koyoharu Gotouge/SHUEISHA Inc.

© 2021 by Koyoharu Gotouge/SHUEISHA Inc.

© 2021 by Koyoharu Gotouge/SHUEISHA Inc.

© 2021 by Koyoharu Gotouge/SHUEISHA Inc.

© 2021 by Koyoharu Gotouge/SHUEISHA Inc.

© 2021 by Koyoharu Gotouge/SHUEISHA Inc.

© 2021 by Koyoharu Gotouge/SHUEISHA Inc.

© 2021 by Koyoharu Gotouge/SHUEISHA Inc.

© 2021 by Koyoharu Gotouge/SHUEISHA Inc.

© 2021 by Koyoharu Gotouge/SHUEISHA Inc.

© 2021 by Koyoharu Gotouge/SHUEISHA Inc.

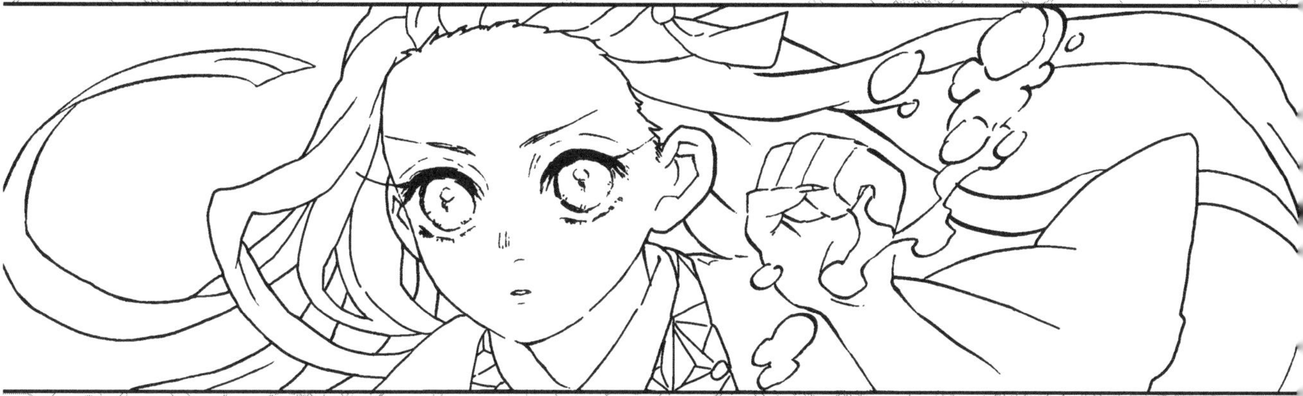
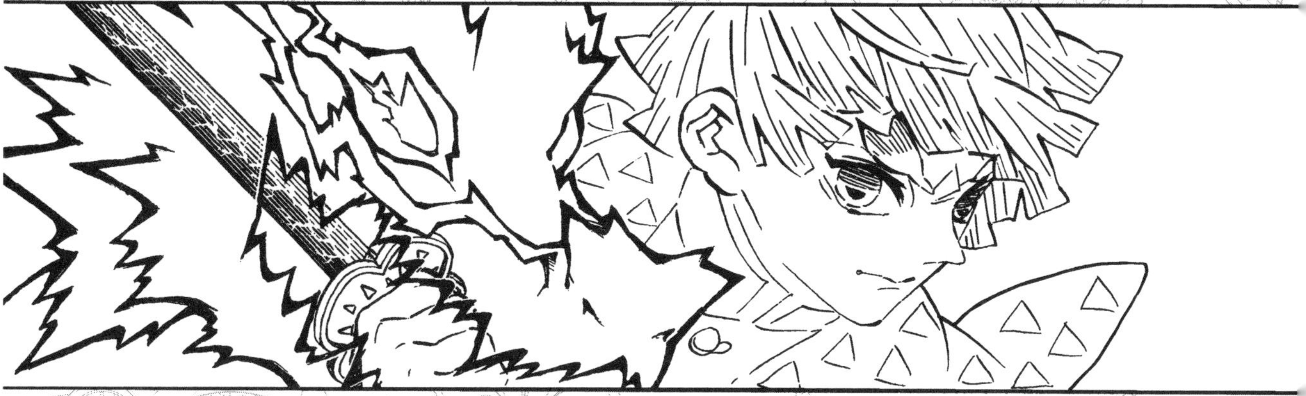
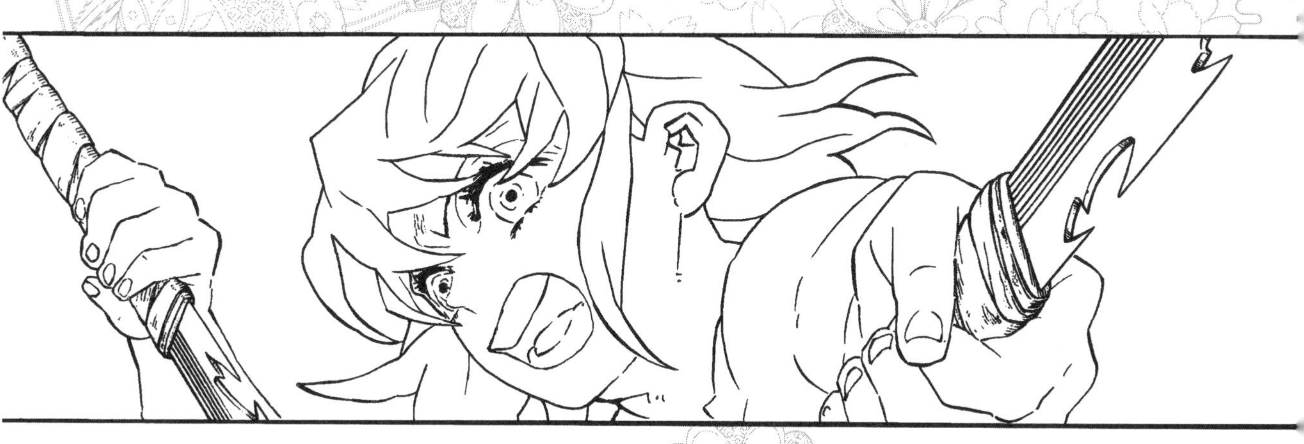

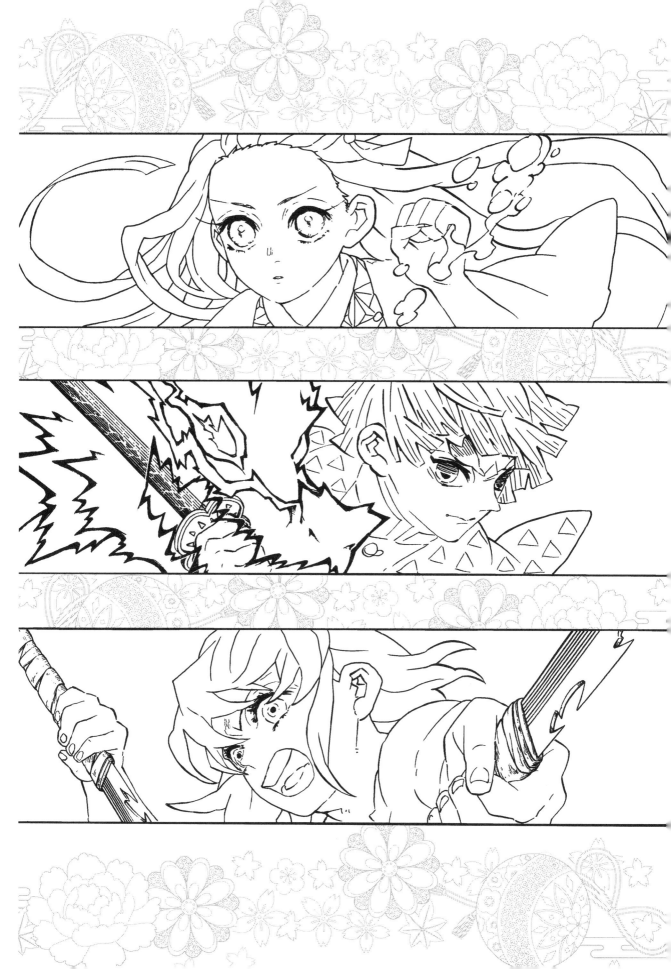

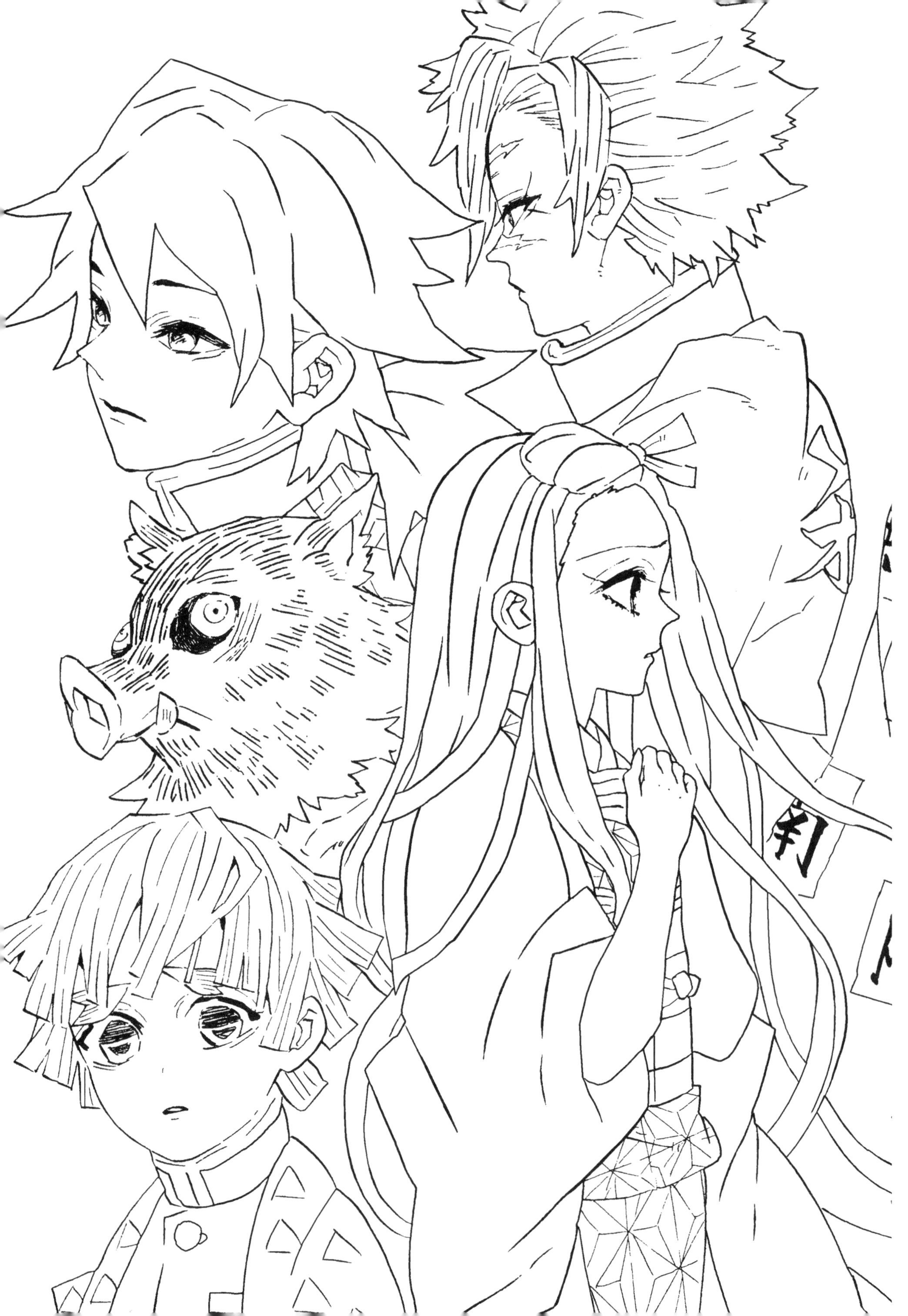

© 2021 by Koyoharu Gotouge/SHUEISHA Inc.

© 2021 by Koyoharu Gotouge/SHUEISHA Inc.

© 2021 by Koyoharu Gotouge/SHUEISHA Inc.

© 2021 by Koyoharu Gotouge/SHUEISHA Inc.

© 2021 by Koyoharu Gotouge/SHUEISHA Inc.

© 2021 by Koyoharu Gotouge/SHUEISHA Inc.
Text is read right to left.

© 2021 by Koyoharu Gotouge/SHUEISHA Inc.

© 2021 by Koyoharu Gotouge/SHUEISHA Inc.

© 2021 by Koyoharu Gotouge/SHUEISHA Inc.

© 2021 by Koyoharu Gotouge/SHUEISHA Inc.

© 2021 by Koyoharu Gotōge/SHUEISHA Inc.

© 2021 by Koyoharu Gotouge/SHUEISHA Inc.

© 2021 by Koyoharu Gotouge/SHUEISHA Inc.

© 2021 by Koyoharu Gotouge/SHUEISHA Inc.

© 2021 by Koyoharu Gotouge/SHUEISHA Inc.

© 2021 by Koyoharu Gotouge/SHUEISHA Inc.

© 2021 by Koyoharu Gotouge/SHUEISHA Inc.

© 2021 by Koyoharu Gotouge/SHUEISHA Inc.

© 2021 by Koyoharu Gotouge/SHUEISHA Inc.

© 2021 by Koyoharu Gotouge/SHUEISHA Inc.

© 2021 by Koyoharu Gotouge/SHUEISHA Inc.

© 2021 by Koyoharu Gotouge/SHUEISHA Inc.

© 2021 by Koyoharu Gotouge/SHUEISHA Inc.

© 2021 by Koyoharu Gotouge/SHUEISHA Inc.

© 2021 by Koyoharu Gotouge/SHUEISHA Inc.

© 2021 by Koyoharu Gotouge/SHUEISHA Inc.

FWEEET

© 2021 by Koyoharu Gotouge/SHUEISHA Inc.

© 2021 by Koyoharu Gotouge/SHUEISHA Inc.

© 2021 by Koyoharu Gotouge/SHUEISHA Inc.

© 2021 by Koyoharu Gotouge/SHUEISHA Inc.

© 2021 by Koyoharu Gotouge/SHUEISHA Inc.

© 2021 by Koyoharu Gotouge/SHUEISHA Inc.

© 2021 by Koyoharu Gotouge/SHUEISHA Inc.

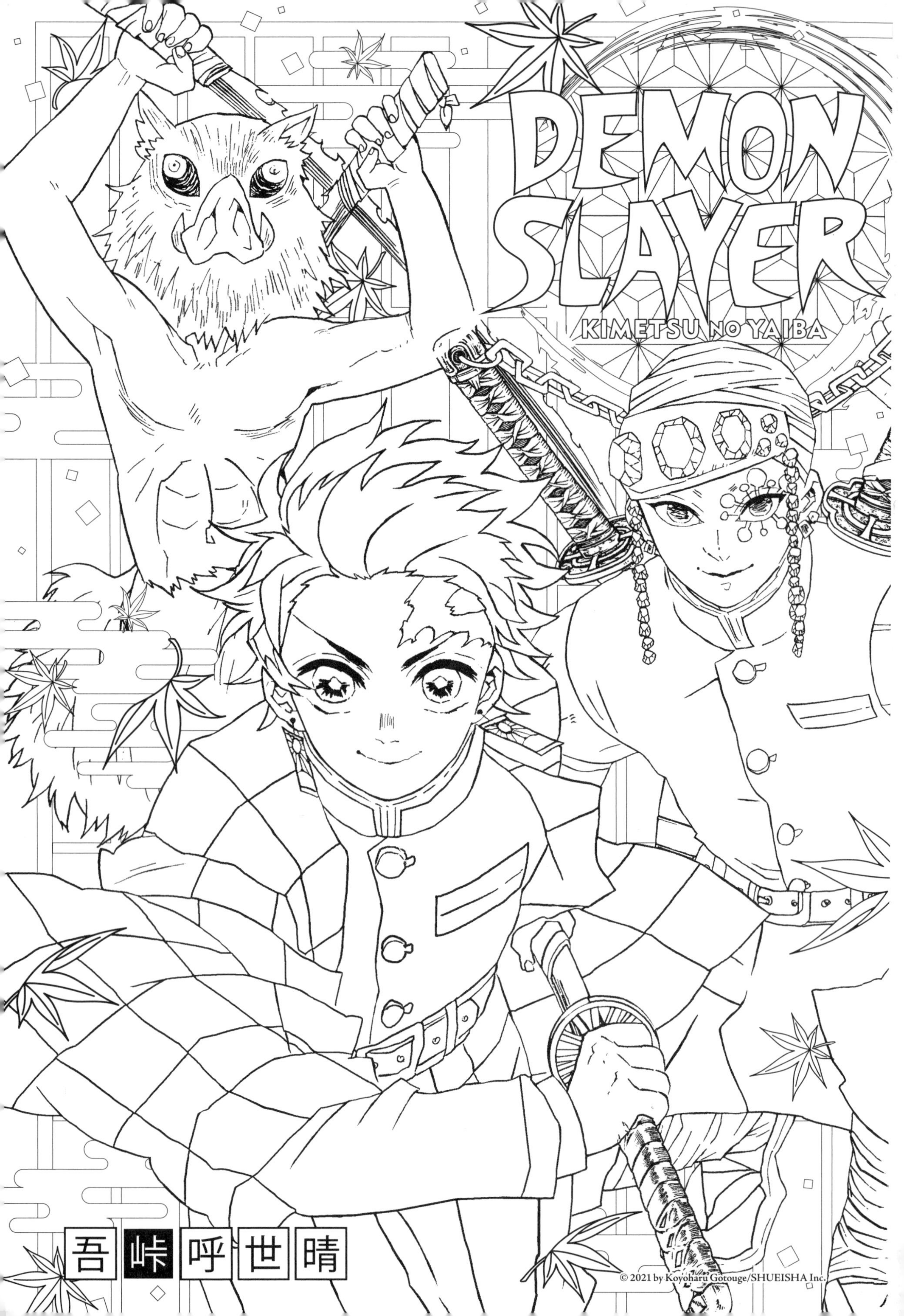
DEMON SLAYER
KIMETSU NO YAIBA
吾峠呼世晴